'CUBA WILL NEVER ADOPT CAPITALIST METHODS'

Cuba's Rectification Process
The Victory In Angola
Over Apartheid's Army

Fidel Castro

PATHFINDER
NEW YORK   LONDON   MONTREAL   SYDNEY

Copyright © 1988 by Pathfinder Press
All rights reserved

ISBN 978-0-87348-538-8
Library of Congress Control Number 2012939035

Manufactured in Canada

First edition, 1988
Twelfth printing, 2025

PATHFINDER
pathfinderpress.com
Email: pathfinder@pathfinderpress.com

CONTENTS

Preface
Michael Taber — 5

CUBA WILL NEVER ADOPT CAPITALIST METHODS
Fidel Castro — 9

Notes — 47

Preface

THIS PAMPHLET CONTAINS the July 26, 1988, speech by Cuban President Fidel Castro in Santiago de Cuba, Cuba's second largest city, and the center of Santiago de Cuba Province on the southeastern part of the island.

Major portions from the speech are included, focusing on Cuba's rectification process and the role of Cuban troops in the historic victory won in early 1988 in southern Angola against invading troops of the South African apartheid regime.

In the opening of his speech, not reprinted here, Castro reviews the accomplishments of the working people of Santiago de Cuba Province in advancing industrial and agricultural development, education, and health care. The province is also an area with a very large number of Cubans of African descent.

As Castro notes, it was in Santiago de Cuba that the revolutionary movement he helped found launched the July 26, 1953, assault on the Moncada garrison, which, although unsuccessful, opened the battle to bring down the dictatorship of Fulgencio Batista. In December 1956, Castro and eighty-one other revolutionaries landed in southeastern Cuba aboard the small yacht *Granma* and established their guerrilla front in the Sierra Maestra mountains.

Throughout the revolutionary war that followed, the working people of what is now Santiago de Cuba Province played a leading role in waging strikes, holding demonstrations, attacking Batista's forces, and launching other struggles in support of the July 26 Movement, as the forces led by Castro became known.

The people of Santiago de Cuba have also been in the vanguard in promoting the rectification process, Castro explains in the speech. Rectification is how the Cubans refer to the political campaign led by the Communist Party of Cuba to uproot the bureaucratism, inefficiency, corruption, and privilege that had begun to infect the revolution in the 1970s.

As Castro had explained previously, the Cuban revolution began to go off course when it increasingly counted on the blind functioning of economic mechanisms and plans to build socialism, rather than political mobilization and deepening the communist consciousness of the working class. Productivity and work quality began to decline; construction projects were started but never finished; the voluntary work brigades that characterized the early years of the revolution were abandoned. A social layer of administrators and functionaries grew up who began to act like capitalists. They counterposed their individual well-being to the social needs of Cuban working people as a whole, and believed the only way to motivate workers was by showering them with unearned bonuses and special privileges.

In the speech below, Castro sharply assails those in Cuba who favor use of capitalist mechanisms—which appeal to workers on the basis of material self-interest—instead of the communist leadership methods being applied today through rectification. He points to the achievements of the volunteer work brigades, which have been revived and are shaking up all of Cuban society with a whirlwind of construction of child-care centers, clinics, roads, bridges, and housing.

The rectification process was launched out of the 1986 Third Congress of the Communist Party of Cuba. Several meetings mentioned by Castro below showed the progress registered since 1986, including the July 6–7, 1988, convention of the National Union of Construction Workers; a July 7–8, 1988, meeting of administrators, union leaders, and party and youth representatives from Havana factories and offices (called "enterprises"); and the July 14–15, 1988, meeting of the Central Committee of the Communist Party of Cuba.

In the final portion of this speech, Castro describes the momentous decisions made by the Cuban government in early 1988 when a South African offensive directed at Cuito Cuanavale, Angola, threatened a major defeat for troops of the Angolan government. The Cuban leadership not only sent thousands of soldiers to reinforce the Cuban troops already fighting in Angola, but reduced Cuba's own antiaircraft defenses by shipping its most modern weapons to Angola. Cuban and Angolan troops, together with South West Africa People's Organisation (SWAPO) forces, inflicted a stunning defeat on the apartheid army, reversing the relationship of forces throughout southern Africa. This would have been impossible without Cuba's role. The victory also forced South Africa to withdraw its troops from Angola and to sit down at the negotiating table, where discussions are currently under way for obtaining the independence of Namibia.

Shortly before this speech was given, a three-part TV

documentary was shown in Cuba, "Response to the South African Escalation," with footage of the combat in Angola. It was so popular that it was rebroadcast twice.

The documentary included several clips of Castro himself, in which he explained that "Africa's history will have one very important moment. But it must be written before Cuito Cuanavale and after Cuito Cuanavale, because the powerful South Africans, the whites, the superior race, smashed up against a small piece of territory defended by Blacks and mulattos—I call all Cubans mulattos—from Angola and the Caribbean."

The translation below is a revised version of the text published in the August 7, 1988, English-language *Granma Weekly Review*.

Michael Taber
NOVEMBER 1988

Cuba will never adopt capitalist methods

BY FIDEL CASTRO

EVEN THOUGH WE KNOW we're just beginning, the first fruits of the policy of rectification of errors and negative tendencies are already being seen. We were able to appreciate it at the construction workers' congress held recently in Havana. There was a marked change in the construction workers' mentality and spirit. We already know that a construction project cannot be prolonged indefinitely. We already know that when a project is started it must be finished. The people of Santiago de Cuba have given us a good lesson on this.

I was able to see that spirit at the Havana Province and City of Havana Province enterprise meeting, attended by representatives of more than 1,000 enterprises. There were notable changes in two years: from a situation in which there was no control whatsoever, distorted wages, chaos; to a situation in which concepts of accounting, of cost, of efficiency are starting to appear.

Those of us who have had the privilege of participating in all three meetings—the first, two years ago; the second, a year ago; and the third, held recently—have been able to see the profound changes that have taken place in the mentality of administrative and technical personnel. Certain really new, necessary, essential ideas are making headway: the need to apply scientific techniques in the organization and management of enterprises; broadly defined jobs; and an appropriate concept of seniority, wherein years of service are not an essential element to assign a post, but where the essential element is qualification, and where the years of service should be taken into account when two workers have the same qualifications.

With excessive paternalism and as a legacy of the old concepts and clashes between workers and capitalists, socialism everywhere—and in our country as well—led to a number of soft standards and a series of concessions that became real obstacles to the development of the productive forces.

Recently, we saw an outstanding example of what it means to apply the concept of broadly defined jobs when we opened the country's largest thermoelectric plant in Matanzas Province, with a 300,000-kilowatt capacity. According to traditional standards, 531 workers were supposedly needed there; applying this concept, the plant is working with less than 249 workers. The payroll was cut down to less than half. Imagine how much we save in transportation, in dining rooms, in everything—even in offices, because the big office that was planned for the plant according to the old concept is being used as an engineering school for 200 students. Imagine the size of the office! And there is still enough room for the office workers that were to work there.

But it's not only a matter of cutting down the number of office workers, but of reducing the number of workers in the production units. There is enormous potential to raise the level of efficiency and productivity in our factories, and this must be applied not only to production centers, but to service centers as well.

These ideas that are gaining ground are really promising in terms of efficient and highly productive work.

We don't want anyone to be jobless on the street. When the day comes that we work well, with efficiency, and there is a surplus labor force, the solution then will lie in reducing the workday. But beware of thinking about this for the time being, don't even dream of it! On the contrary, now is when we have to work the most.

What did we tell the construction workers who are going to build the Baconao dam? That they would have to work day and night, in two twelve-hour shifts.

What did we tell the workers who are going to build the overpass? And I forgot to mention the project that we're also going to speed up, connecting the new airport with important areas of the city. I have also failed to mention that construction feat—Santiago de Cuba's new airport—a sort of aircraft carrier along the entire coast; they are filling in the cliff that was there to make an international airport with a four-kilometer-long runway. Well, the overpass is already being built, Santiago de Cuba's overpass—construction was going on at a slow pace because they needed some equipment, but that was solved. What did we tell those comrades? Organize a contingent and work day and night, like those who built the stone road for the oil industry in Cárdenas Bay, or better yet, like the handful of workers who have just built the twenty-kilometer-long stone road from Turiguanó to Cayo Coco, in Ciego de Avila, in only fifteen or sixteen months. And through shallow waters they have joined the coast with an island that has great possibilities for tourism, located more than twenty kilometers away from the coast. Quietly, silently, they started in March and today we received news sent by the construction workers saying that either yesterday or today—I'm not sure when—they had joined the mainland with Cayo Coco in tribute to July 26. [*Applause*]

What we now tell everyone is that we must work hard, we must make good use of those machines. If a bulldozer costs $100,000, there's not much point in using it five or six hours. If it costs $100,000, we must have it working fifteen or twenty hours every day, and the bulldozer won't have any problems if it's handled properly and given good upkeep.

We told the comrades: we don't have many bulldozers or loaders, so we must get the most from that equipment. We are telling the people who will build highways for the city, aqueducts for the city, agricultural projects for the city that you must work hard and work a lot.

Perhaps one of the tragedies of Third World countries is that they long for the level of consumption of the developed capitalist countries, working seven, six, or five hours. That is a dream, an illusion. If we want great material riches—those we need and those we want—then we must work and work hard, we must increase labor productivity, we must make rational use of all human and material resources. There is no other way.

In recent days I was amazed to read some news reports that in Japan—the capitalist country that has advanced most in the last period, the most industrialized capitalist country, which has surpassed the United States and the European Community and other mighty industrial sectors in the world—I read a dispatch saying the Japanese have an average of six vacation days a year, six days!

I'm not proposing that Cubans have six days of vacation. We already have some bad habits that won't be easy to change; I'm not proposing so much. I'm proposing that we work as hard as we have to on the work days of the year.[1] [*Applause*] If you add up the month of vacation, the nonworking Saturday, the working Saturday that is half nonworking for some people, plus absenteeism under any pretext and narrowly defined jobs in factories, we find that people are not actually working eight, seven-and-a-half, or even seven hours. It's less. It would be demagogic and irresponsible to tell the people or any citizen that a country can develop and obtain everything it needs by working deficiently or working little.

Of course with those narrowly defined jobs, it is hard to find things for some people to fill eight hours with. One of the main things about the process of rectification is the studies we have undertaken, the ideas being worked out for implementation in some new workplaces, since we don't want to create political problems. For if we were to apply this rigorously in all workplaces, we would have an excess of workers, and what we want to do is to use all the surplus workers in a rational and useful manner and not create traumas. For if someone is told he is not needed in his job, even if he's sent home with full pay, he'll be traumatized, and we don't want to solve problems that way. We don't want to traumatize anybody. But there are great possibilities if we are capable of implementing these principles.

We don't impose anything on workers, we persuade workers. We say, this is in your interest as a citizen, in the interest of your fellow workers and of your country, of your homeland and your people. We use persuasion, not command. Issuing orders is easy; what's difficult is to do things with intelligent, political methods. Often this obliges us to go slowly, but it is better to go slowly, because, you go further than if you run and don't get very far, or get nowhere, or have to turn back.

I think that very important possibilities are opening up for our country, and what we are seeing here in the provinces shows it.

I mentioned the meeting of enterprises in the capital. I could also mention the meeting of the Central Committee of the party, where the state agencies reported on what they were doing and the results they were getting in the process of rectification. Or I could mention the last meeting of the National Assembly, where the reports from the provinces were really encouraging, impressive, where progress is being made.

The years 1987 and 1988 have been very difficult ones and possibly the next two or three years will be the hardest of the revolution in terms of hard currency, as we have explained, because the prices of our basic exports dropped and the currencies of countries from which we buy became more expensive. Because the drought reduced sugar output by more than a million tons, and not only have we had to reduce to almost zero our sugar exports to the countries that pay in hard currency, but we've also had to purchase a million tons of sugar a year to fulfill our commitments to the socialist countries. A million tons of sugar imported annually during these years of drought! Never before has the revolution had more problems with hard currency, never!

In other times what we purchased had different prices, and there was credit. When there was drought and other problems there was always a solution to find the hard currency; now there is none, now we must pay cash for virtually everything.

We have our trade with the socialist countries, which is normal: we supply them and they supply us. But we have very serious hard currency problems. However, we will see what can be done. We will see what can be done to reduce imports, save hard currency, and increase exports.

That's why at the Central Committee meeting we said that since the rains in May, June, and July have been good, we had to take advantage of the opportunity, weed all the cane, that we couldn't speak of vacations while there was unweeded cane. We have asked agricultural workers to make a special effort, especially sugarcane growers, so that it can all be weeded in July and August. This can mean the hundreds of thousands of additional tons of sugar that the country needs.

The sugar workers' response has been excellent. More than 200,000 of them are in the fields weeding the cane, amidst the rigors of summer, the sun, and July and August heat. We can't live in a dream world, we can't ignore reality. If we can obtain another 500,000 tons of sugar, then we can't go off to relax and have fun. That's why I said there was an excellent response everywhere.

We are doing many things, much more than what we did when the amount of imports from the capitalist countries was incomparably greater. That's why we must develop exports in every possible branch and exploit two marvelous resources of the country, the sun and the sea. That's why we must develop tourism and are making a special effort in this field.

There is a great international demand for tourist accommodations in Cuba and you know about the wonders of our coasts and nature. There is Baconao Park, for example. There you can see what's been done in a short time with limited means, and there are three international hotels in Baconao bringing in hard currency.

Some people will say: "It's too bad I can't go to such and such hotel." But we can't have everything. We can't have waterworks, schools, hospitals, health, food, transportation, everything, and in addition enjoy all the hotels. We have no choice but to export hotel services and deprive ourselves of some hotels. Although often during part of the year when there is no international tourism, especially in the hot months, those hotels will provide service for Cubans—except in the case of joint enterprises, where that would mean a loss of hard currency for the country.

I say this because there are people who react unrealistically. I have heard petty-bourgeois, genuinely petty-bourgeois views from people who want to have the university, hospital, school, career, job, transportation, recreation, art, culture, everything! They say: "It really bothers me that in my country I can't go to such and such a hotel," which they view as a tragedy and the fault of the revolution. We could also say, "It's too bad we can't consume all the lobster we produce!" We produce more than 10,000 tons of lobster and we must export it to rich Japanese, to rich Spaniards, to rich Canadians, so they can eat lobster while we go without. It is very tasty, no one doubts that, and it is served in some restaurants.

There may be no lobster, but the price of a ton of lobster on the world market enables us to buy 20 tons of powdered milk, and with those 20 tons we produce 200,000 liters of milk, and those 200,000 liters provide milk all year long for many children in the mountains, many who never had milk before, many who were formerly undernourished. [*Applause*] We can say there is no lobster on the Cuban menu, but there are no children begging in the streets. [*Applause*] There is no lobster, but there are no undernourished or starving children in our country. All children get a liter of milk daily, which is why we have one of the healthiest peoples in the world. [*Applause*]

We can indeed say, let us export our lobster to make certain that we have the milk, beans, chick-peas, and the feed we need to produce eggs, poultry, and other food. Or would we rather eat our lobster and give up, fail to get more than $100 million? Afterward we would not have spare parts for anything, raw materials for medicines, surgical equipment, X-rays. And then when the day comes that we need all this, when a member of our family needs all this, that'll be the day when we're truly sorry that we lacked the medicine, when we lack the disposable material for an operation, the day when it comes time to save his life or restore his health.

Some people still can't understand that, they can't understand we must exploit our sunshine—and even our moonlight—shining down on us today. We're not living on the North Pole or on the South Pole, we're not living in a cold country; we live in a hot country, more so here in Santiago de Cuba.

That's one asset. Others have oil and they exploit it, export it. Much of that money went to an unknown destination. Very often it was wasted. But our wealth doesn't come easily, we must work very hard to get it. It's not easy to grow sugarcane, it's not easy to produce sugar—luckily, we have now mechanized that process in the harvest—and we must work hard to earn our bread, to get those resources.

Exports are hard and there's tough competition also in the field of tourism. Now tourism can be a source of employment for tens of thousands of our compatriots who must all be qualified workers, who must know how to treat tourists the way they should be treated. So, we're going to develop tourism, and in everything that concerns national hotels or enterprises controlled by the country, in the absence of foreign tourists, we can use these during the hot months for Cuban tourists. But, of course, it would be an illusion to imagine that we're going to have a room in a tourist resort on every beach in the country for 10 million Cubans in the months of July and August.

Being very realistic and with plenty of common sense, we're developing our camping plans, for we must turn tourism into one of the sources of foreign exchange income for the country. And I think that in this the people of Santiago de Cuba ought to be in the forefront. The traditionally hospitable city of Santiago must occupy a prominent place in tourism. We're building new hotels in Baconao and we're also going to build new hotels over there in the west. [*Applause*]

Naturally, many of the good things we have for foreign tourists are also enjoyed by the population. If we build an aquarium the whole population enjoys it and so do the tourists; if we build a zoo the whole population will enjoy it and so will the tourists; if we build children's and young people's recreational centers, like those we have in Baconao, all the children enjoy them. This tourist development is also going to help the population in many things and will bring the country substantial income.

I believe this is another of the ambitious plans we must boost in the province of Santiago de Cuba. And I think that the people understand it, the proletarian understands it, the worker understands it—but the petty bourgeois does not understand it. And we still have spoiled young people here who have been raised in a petty-bourgeois environment and as such are far removed from reality. That's the truth. [*Applause*]

We must continue making new efforts in this process. I was explaining how, in spite of the acute shortage of foreign exchange, we are making more things than in past years and our economy is growing. The Santiago de Cuba economy grew by more than 7 percent in this six-month period, and the economy of nearly all the provinces grew by 4, 5, 6 percent, in spite of all the difficulties—and growing genuinely, mind you, not creating phony figures. You accomplish nothing in a factory that has ninety different lines and only makes forty and gets so many millions with just forty. What good does that do if it does not make the other fifty? Or else, make so many millions from buildings that are never finished. What good do they do other than waste cement, fuel, materials? Our economy is growing in spite of the drought we had last year. It must keep on growing. In spite of all these difficulties, we must really manage to do things better and increasingly solve our problems and solve them better. This is what the rectification process is all about.

It's not just us. We all know because we read in the papers that other socialist countries are analyzing their history, their performance, their work; they're trying to overcome their difficulties. There's never been a period in history in which a social regime, a social system, has in such a short time achieved such huge accomplishments as socialism has. Yet when it comes to any human endeavor, there will always be material for criticism, for analysis, and for overcoming the difficulties. A revolutionary never feels satisfied, nor can he ever feel that way; he must be eternally dissatisfied.

It was following the Third Congress of our party, which very realistically, clearly, and courageously analyzed our difficulties, our mistakes, and our negative tendencies, that this process of rectification began. More or less simultaneously, the same thing happened in the Soviet Union and in other socialist countries, without anyone having agreed to do so beforehand.

There are some people who believe that what's being done in other places is what we ought to start doing right away. And there are also some brains around—people who have no confidence in themselves, no confidence in their nation, no confidence in their people, no confidence in their revolution—who right away say we have to copy what others are doing. [*Applause*] That's an incorrect viewpoint, a wrong viewpoint, because no two revolutionary processes are the same, no two countries are the same, no two histories are the same, no two characteristics are the same. Some have certain problems, others have different problems; some make certain mistakes, others make different mistakes.

If someone has a toothache, why would he take a cure for corns? Or if his corns hurt, why must he take a cure for a toothache? That's why our measures are not the same, nor can they be the same as those used by other countries. It would be entirely wrong for us to look for the same solutions or mechanically copy the other countries' solutions.

One thing I ought to say here: this revolution has been characterized not by being a copier but by being a creator.

[*Applause*] Had we been willing to follow the schemas, we would not be gathered here today, we would not have had a July 26, we would not have had a socialist revolution in this hemisphere—perhaps there would not have been any yet. Had we been willing to follow the schemas, theory had it that no revolution could be made here; that's what the theory used to say, that's what the books used to say, what the manuals used to say. Let it be well understood: that's what the theory, the books, the manuals used to say!

Our situation was no worse than that of other Latin American countries. Cuba's objective economic and social conditions, however bad they were—and they were indeed bad—did not resemble the objective conditions of other Latin American countries much worse off. And today we see that no socialist revolution has yet been made in those countries.

I make one exception here—and I'm not placing it in the category of a socialist revolution but in whatever category they may wish to place it in, although I consider it a true and profound revolution—I make the exception of the Nicaraguan revolution. [*Applause*] It is up to them alone to know how things should be done there, how problems should be tackled.

Recently, Daniel [Ortega] spoke about the essence, the character, or the socialist sense of the Nicaraguan revolution. That caused a lot of noise, and he was only speaking about the essence, the character, the sense of the process. He did not say it was a socialist revolution.

So there have been no other ones in the rest of Latin America, where all the problems that I was mentioning here remain. There are some places where every year 100 children die per 1,000 live births, and in some other places the number is 150 and even 200. In a very few countries infant mortality is below 60. Prostitution, drugs, begging, poverty are everywhere. Rickets, malnutrition, children without schools, young people unemployed and without universities are everywhere and there's been no revolution.

A revolution depends on many circumstances and making one is not easy in any sense.

Had we said: let's wait for a huge economic crisis to break out in Cuba, like the one under dictator Machado[2] or even worse than that one, and let starvation drive people to rise up, we would still be waiting. But we drew our own conclusions starting from the principles of socialism, of Marxism-Leninism—not from the pamphlets—and we said: there are objective conditions in Cuba for a revolution; what's missing are subjective conditions. Our people have special characteristics. The subjective conditions for the revolution could be created because there were objective conditions present.

It wasn't a whim, for we were thinking about the revolution even before March 10, 1952.[3] We would have tried to follow the revolutionary path with or without March 10. I meant it because there were some of us thinking about a true revolution even before March 10, [*Applause*] and about a revolution with the people, about a profound revolution, about a revolution that sooner or later had to become a socialist revolution—for we could not conceive of a different type of revolution in our country, dominated by neocolonialism, dominated by imperialism; in this country where nearly all the sugar mills, railroads, mines, ports, best lands, electricity, telephones, rubber, everything, belonged to foreigners. We were but a colony, worse than a colony!

Starting out from two currents of thought, starting

out—to be more exact—from Marxist-Leninist thought and Martí's thought,[4] starting out from a true appraisal of our people, their characteristics, their history, the objective realities that afflicted them, even if they were not as bad as those that afflicted other countries on our continent, we arrived at the conclusion that the revolution was possible in our country. This is why our country, which was the last one—the last one!—to free itself from Spain, became the first one to free itself from U.S. imperialism in this hemisphere, the first one! And the first one to carry out a socialist revolution. [*Applause*]

I'd like to know what some of those second-rate copiers and imitators would have done under circumstances similar to those that existed here before July 26. We could place them in similar circumstances from where our revolution started out and see what they'd do.

That's why I say that the first major test that showed that ours was a creative revolution is that it did not follow the schemas and that in constructing socialism our revolution made many contributions while remaining faithful to the principles of Marxism-Leninism. One example for instance is the principle of combining study and work proclaimed by [Karl] Marx stemming from the history of the British working class, whose exploited children were turned into a productive force. Marx conceived the idea that under socialism study and work could and should be combined; and Martí, on the basis of his familiarity with our people's characteristics and reality, said the same thing. Our country was the first one in the world to massively and consistently apply those principles and today we see the fruits in the behavior of our youth, because it's not by chance that our new generations display the revolutionary attributes we see in them.

This principle has been applied for the past twenty-five years. We already have whole generations—every young person thirty-five years old or under has in one way or another taken part in programs combining study and work. That's why when called upon to join a particular project, or do voluntary work, they are not afraid. That was proof of our revolution's creative spirit.

The powerful mass organizations created by our revolution also attested to that creative spirit: the Committees for the Defense of the Revolution, the Federation of Cuban Women, the peasants' organization—not as committees at the top but as grass-roots organizations—were created by the revolution. I'm not talking about something that already existed like the workers organized in trade unions. No other revolution had the mass organization that our revolution had, organizations that other revolutions that came later tried to utilize as an example. The Committees for the Defense of the Revolution now exist in several Third World countries that have made their own revolutions.

The manner in which an agrarian reform was carried out in our country differed from the manner in which all the other socialist countries carried it out, because they all divided up the land and we didn't. Had we divided up the big cattle ranches or the sugar plantations in small lots or tiny parcels, today we would not be supplying calories for 40 million people. We kept those land units intact and developed them as big production enterprises. We gave land to the peasant who was in possession of it, to sharecroppers, tenant farmers, and others. We said to them all, here you are, the land is yours, and subsequently we have not forced any of them to join cooperatives. The process of uniting those plots has taken us thirty years. We've gone ahead little by little on the basis of the strict principle of it being voluntary. There is not a single peasant in Cuba who can say that he was forced to join a cooperative, there is not a single one! And yet, more than two-thirds of their lands now belong to cooperatives, and all of them are making headway, they are prospering. On the other hand, 80 percent of the land in our country belongs to state farms that even collectively produce their own food. The cooperatives also produce their own food. Ours was a different road.

Our revolution—and this no one can deny—has been kept going with tremendous ideological strength, because who can defend us here? Were imperialism to attack us, who is there to defend the island? No one will come from abroad to defend our island; we defend the island ourselves. [*Applause*] It's not that someone might not want to defend us, but that no one can, because this socialist revolution is not just a few kilometers away from the Soviet Union; this socialist revolution is 10,000 kilometers away from the Soviet Union.

Were the revolutionary process in Cuba to suffer a crisis, who would save it? Will imperialism come to save the revolutionary process? Were the revolutionary process in Cuba to be weakened, who would save it?

That's why all that we do has exceptional importance. It's not that we want to be more virtuous than anybody else or purer than anybody else, but we are ninety miles away from the most powerful empire on earth and 10,000 kilometers away from the socialist camp. We are two millimeters away from the empire, right there at the Guantánamo naval base and that's why the empire is trying to weaken the revolution ideologically. That's why it is campaigning so much, making so much propaganda, to try to sow distrust, doubt, division, weaken the revolution, and swallow it up like a ripe apple. That's what they said in centuries past and they devised the theory of the ripe apple. But they have not succeeded despite all their planning and plotting, nor will they succeed in undermining it from within.

That's why I can only feel contempt for those who allow themselves to be carried away by silly things and illusions, those with a weak heart, a weak brain, a weak will, who are unable to grasp these realities.

I believe that our country has carried out an extraordinary historic feat in building socialism in the geographical conditions in which it has done so and that's why we must watch over the ideological purity of the revolution, the ideological solidity of the revolution. [*Applause*] That's why we cannot use mechanisms, any kind of tools smacking of capitalism; this is an essential question of the revolution's survival. That's why the revolution must resolutely stick to the purest principles of Marxism-Leninism and Martí's thought, stick to them rather than playing around or flirting with the things of capitalism.

We believe in socialism and do so deeply! [*Applause*] Because socialism has changed our nation, socialism has changed our lives, and socialism promises to do a lot more. Because the fact that we can speak today about these and other things—housing, shantytowns that can be demolished in no time, water, food, education and health for all, industrial and agricultural development—is because we are the owners of our country. Socialism made us the owners of our lands, our sugar mills, our factories, our mines, of everything, and that's why we can say: let's get to work, let's do this or the other, anything. Could we do this in a capitalist society or in a caricature of capitalism like this country used to be, in a Yankee neocolony?

We believe in socialism and, therefore, we must be very careful when interpreting and applying the theory; we must be very careful in every step we take. And the revolution was always like that, it is now almost thirty and it looks healthy, full of pep, strong, ninety miles from the United States. [*Applause*]

That's why each country, on the basis of its own history and concrete experiences, must draw up its own formulas, and we respect the formulas drawn up by each country. We have the fullest respect for them. We are glad for the efforts being made by the socialist countries to overcome their difficulties, the problems that have been created for them throughout history. Yet there are many problems that arose in the other countries that did not arise in ours. Our problems are different, of another type, precisely because we do not copy from others, because we were creative and did not simply copy from others.

On occasion I've even criticized our having had so much zeal for applying our own interpretations that we neglected using the positive experiences of the socialist countries. But occasionally we also copied negative experiences of the socialist countries, and that's the truth. Now we'll go on searching for our own path, our own formulas; we'll always go on paying attention to what any socialist country does that can be useful to us, and we'll go on being reluctant to abjectly copy prescriptions to remedy ills we've never been afflicted with. And, needless to say, we not only wish but need the socialist countries to succeed in their efforts to overcome their difficulties, and I trust they'll be successful, for I've never been a pessimist. I have great confidence in socialism and I believe we all do because we have proof and reasons for that confidence.

I believe that socialism has accomplished extraordinary things—what the Soviet Union did has no precedent, what the Soviet people did has no precedent, starting with the Great October Revolution; their resistance against a generalized invasion by all the capitalist countries following World War I; their industrialization; their resistance against fascism; the 20 million lives they lost in saving socialism and saving humanity from fascism; a country that had hardly been constructed when it was destroyed and they rebuilt it again; a country that achieved nuclear parity with imperialism, an incredible feat; a country whose spaceships are right now headed for the moons of Mars.

We're familiar with their successes. Can more be achieved? Yes, it can. Must we try to do better? Of course. But we do not deny nor will we ever permit others to deny the colossal successes achieved by socialism. I say this because the imperialists, on the basis of the self-criticism now going on in the socialist countries and the Soviet Union, are bent on discrediting everything that socialism has accomplished. They're trying to discredit everything that socialism has done, to detract from the historical merits of socialism, and to demoralize it.

If I were asked, I have my own opinion about what its flaws are, and some of them I have thought over many times. But it is not up to me to proclaim the problems of others because each country has to analyze and solve its own problems. I could even say what equipment has difficulties, but I can also speak about many good and marvelous things about socialist technology and socialist equipment. Those cane harvesters, for instance, the thousands of cane harvesters we now have that were designed and manufactured with the cooperation of the Soviet Union and with which we have reduced the number of canecutters from 350,000 to 70,000. [*Applause*]

Of course we can make them better, and we're trying to make them better and more productive; with hydraulic and nonmechanical mechanisms, we're trying to do all that. We're already manufacturing a second-generation harvester and will later start with the third. And eventually we will have increasingly better harvesters, starting with that factory and those machines supplied to us by the Soviet Union.

Our country is producing sugar mill tandems and is manufacturing nearly 60 percent of our sugar mills in the machine plants supplied to us by the Soviet Union. Here in Santiago de Cuba our country increased the capacity of this refinery to 3.7 million tons and regenerates the fuel and lubricants with Soviet technology. It is producing lubricants, plastic grease, and naphtha, and will be turning out 180,000 tons of oxide asphalt, that is, of much better quality, with which we can pave 2,000 kilometers of roads a year using socialist technology.

Next to it, in Renté, the former Renté, is the Antonio Maceo thermoelectric plant, which with Soviet equipment can generate 500,000 kilowatts, in addition to the one that formerly existed and the previous expansion work. The generators are there for all to see. Thanks to them we have lights and electricity here. And not just thanks to them but also thanks to our trade on a fair basis with the Soviet Union, thanks to the oil it supplies us and that we pay for with the reasonable prices we get from them for our sugar, our nickel, and other products; that is to say, a trade devoid of unequal exchange. I believe that here lies a great historical merit of the Soviet Union.

We have here Cuba's largest textile mill, equipped with Soviet machines, and in Ariguanabo we have the second largest, also modernized with Soviet machines. Practically all the tractors working our lands, a large portion of our means of transportation carrying our commodities and raw materials, and a big part of our construction equipment are all Soviet-made.

Our weapons are Soviet weapons, which we have used to defend our country; [*Applause*] and also Soviet-made are those weapons (surface-to-air missiles, antiaircraft weapons—all effective and modern—the MIG 23s and the T-55 and T-62 tanks) with which our fighters have gloriously fulfilled their internationalist mission in Angola. [*Applause*]

Lined up against us there are capitalist Mirage jets of Western origin; against us is modern military technology, but the Soviet weapons are there in the hands of our present-day *mambí* fighters,[5] who are proving they can outperform the imperialist weapons. [*Applause*]

I say this, I repeat, because the imperialists are trying to reap a good harvest with this process of criticism and self-criticism now going on in the socialist countries and they are bent on sowing demoralization. Many capitalists believe that socialists will have no choice but to adopt methods, styles, and even motivations and certain characteristics of a capitalist nature. They're indulging themselves in this kind of wishful thinking, trying to fish in troubled waters. They're even trying to blame us for the fact that we're not doing things exactly the same way that the Soviets are doing them, in order to create intrigue, to try to divide us.

Of course, it would be in their interest to pit us one against the other or drive a wedge between Cubans and Soviets.

However, never before has our communication been greater. Our communication with the leadership of the Soviet party is excellent, we understand each other perfectly, we speak a frank and clear language, and it has never occurred to us to think that we simply have to copy what the Soviets do. Nor has it occurred to the Soviet leadership to think that we have to copy what they're doing. That's clear.

Returning to the essential idea here: everyone must have the right to do what suits them best.

In this process I am hoping that if the socialist countries make mistakes, they will be capable of correcting them. Because they will unquestionably make mistakes in the process. Yet I'm confident they will try to rectify them. And that's what we said concerning what we're doing: we must be able to rectify not just the mistakes made and the negative tendencies, but also rectify the mistakes we may make in the process of rectification itself!

What I can indeed tell the imperialists and the theoreticians of imperialism is that Cuba will never adopt methods, styles, philosophies or characteristics of capitalism. That I can indeed tell them! [*Applause*] Capitalism has had some technological successes, some successes in organizational experiences that can be used, but nothing more! Socialism and capitalism are two diametrically different things, by definition and by essence.

We're proud of the ideological purity, of the ideological strength of a country that has confronted imperialism. And not just confronted imperialism but a country where hundreds of thousands of its people have fulfilled internationalist missions, a country where one has only to raise his hand and if 10,000 teachers are needed for Nicaragua, all 10,000 teachers turn up to go to Nicaragua; [*Applause*] if doctors are needed, doctors go there; a country that when fighters were needed has always had ten times more fighters willing to fulfill the mission than the number of fighters actually needed.

That's why today, on this thirty-fifth anniversary, one very basic idea is never to forget where we are located. We're not in the Black Sea but in the Caribbean Sea, not ninety miles from Odessa but ninety miles from Miami, with our land bordering on imperialism in an occupied portion of our territory. Our people are responsible for our country and our party is responsible for its policy, its line, its defense.

Our party is aware it can make no mistakes that will weaken it ideologically. That's why in our rectification process the role of the party is not weakened, the role of the party is made stronger. In our rectification process the role of our party becomes increasingly vital. There will be nothing to weaken the party's authority! Without the party no revolution is possible. Without the party no construction of socialism is possible!

We must say here, once and for all, that we need just one party, in the same way that Martí needed just one party to wage the war for Cuban independence, [*Applause*] in the same way that Lenin needed just one party to make the October revolution. I say this to put a halt to the wishful thinking of those who believe we're going to start allowing pocket-size parties. To organize whom? The counterrevolutionaries, the pro-Yankees, the bourgeoisie? No! There's only one party here, and that is the party of our proletarians, our peasants, our students, our workers, our solidly and indestructibly united people. That's the one we have and will have! [*Applause*] I hope that by the time we are celebrating the seventieth anniversary, the hundredth anniversary, history will prove and demonstrate this.

We don't need capitalist political formulas, they're just trash, they're good for nothing, what with their incessant political scheming. I was telling you here how a voting card used to be required to receive medical attention. None of these phenomena exist here now. We have created our own political structure to suit the country, we have not copied it. These are our own political ways to organize People's Power.

As you know—because that's the practice among you—the candidates for each district's People's Power delegate are not proposed by the party.[6] They are proposed by the people gathered in free assemblies in the district and they choose whoever they think best. They can choose up to eight candidates and a minimum of two, and if one of them doesn't get 50 percent, a new round of voting must start. You don't have to tell me—I haven't been able to escape even once from that second round of voting in the elections in my own district. We all know that and we know that the party doesn't pick anyone or propose anyone, it's the people who do it. It is those delegates from the electoral districts who make up the municipal assembly, the ones who set up and constitute the provincial assemblies. Those delegates of the people, nominated by the people, and elected by the people are the ones who make up the National Assembly of People's Power. [*Applause*]

We have to rectify absolutely none of this. Ours is a superdemocratic system, more democratic than all the bourgeois systems of the millionaires, the plutocracy—who are, generally speaking, the real rulers of the capitalist countries.

We have nothing to learn from them and we will not stray one iota from this road, where power originates from the people. You all know how our party emerged from the people, it didn't drop from heaven. And you know how our party members are chosen from among the best in the youth and from among the best workers. That was also an innovation, something absolutely new in the method of creating and broadening out the party and that is very much present in the history of our party, which always made admission into its ranks subject to the will of the masses, the opinion of the masses, the support of the masses. That's why our party stands so close to the masses. [*Applause*]

I know that outside the party there are millions of extraordinary men and women and communists. We're a people of revolutionaries. Yet the party must be made up of a selection of them and it cannot be otherwise because it must be the vanguard. And you know very well what it means to be a member of the party: he or she must be the first in everything when there's a difficult job, an internationalist mission, a sacrifice to be made, a risk to be taken; there the first turn, the first possibility goes to the party member. It's not a party of privileged people but a party built from among the people, whose members must set an example. And when they don't set an example the party sees to it they are expelled from its ranks. [*Applause*]

In this rectification process the party will have increasing strength because, I repeat, socialism cannot be built without the party. Without the party one can build capitalism, which stands for chaos. Capitalism does not need anyone to organize it, it is self-organized with all its barbarities. Socialism is not created by spontaneous generation. Socialism must be built, and the basic builder is the party.

There is another essential point in our rectification process: we will not weaken the role of our plans or the role of our development programs. We are convinced and are very aware of the importance of planning our development, of how important our plans are; our main problem is to draw them up well. But not only that, we must avoid turning the plans into straitjackets. That's why, while we make sure that we are capable of planning well, we must also create the necessary conditions to cope with new problems, new situations, and new possibilities.

When the dengue epidemic broke out, for example, we could not sit and wait for the next five-year plan to come around to purchase the equipment we needed to fight the disease.[7] Immediately, in twenty-four hours, over the phone, we flew it over from wherever it was. And if it wasn't available in a socialist country, we brought it over from Japan, from the Federal Republic of Germany, from wherever the equipment was to be had. The country must always have a certain amount of reserves to give a quick and immediate response to new problems and new situations. This means that we have to improve our ideas as to how to carry out our economic development. But planning and development programs are inherent to socialism, and we cannot allow these ideas to weaken. That's clear and you understand it.

We have spoken of Santiago de Cuba Province's successes and I wonder, and I ask you with all my heart: Could they have been possible without the work of the party? [*Exclamations of "No!"*] All these hundreds of projects, the miracle that has been created, would not have been possible without the party. The administration alone, the state alone, cannot solve these problems; they cannot work these miracles, which are political miracles. And the party does not try to supplant the administration; on the contrary, it tries to strengthen it. It does not try to weaken the state but rather to strengthen it so it can fulfill its tasks. But the administration cannot carry out political tasks, it cannot mobilize and organize the masses. The state cannot carry out purely political, ideological tasks, mobilize the people, direct the mass organizations. Those tasks can be carried out only by the party.

I wonder if the tremendous success the people of Santiago de Cuba are so proud of today would have been possible without the party's leadership; would it have been possible without Comrade Lazo's[8] tenacious, constant, vigorous, intelligent efforts closely linked to the people? [*Exclamations of "No!" and prolonged applause*] We are aware of the role played by the party and its cadres, and how important is the link between the party and the masses, how important is the link between its cadres and the masses.

That's why after seeing all we've seen, we have a good example. Take this mass rally for instance. Could you find anything like it anywhere else? I'm not speaking of its size, I'm mainly speaking of its attention, I'm speaking of its education, I'm speaking of its spirit, I'm speaking of its discipline. [*Applause*]

This is the fruit of the revolution. This is what the work of the party has reaped, despite whatever errors we may have committed, which we are honestly and bravely struggling against. Whatever our mistakes or our weaknesses may be, we'll fight tenaciously and vigorously against them.

I believe that on a day like today—which as I said invited us to reflect and talk about these topics—these are the most essential things that can be said.

There's perhaps one remaining thing I have to talk about, and it's inevitable that I do so. I realized this the day the ceremony took place in Contramaestre, where I was asked about Angola, about how things were going in Angola. That's why I'm going to take up a little of your time to speak of this question.

You will understand that I have to be very careful, that we must try not to touch on sensitive points, for we are now in a process of negotiations. One must be very careful of what one says. Because when involved in these processes of negotiations, one is committed not to make public the steps that are being taken and we wish to do nothing to break this commitment.

Toward the end of last year, a difficult, critical situation was created in Angola. I'm not going to explain what caused it. It is better for history to speak for itself, and I believe that one day history will reveal it all: where the mistakes lay, why those mistakes were made. I shall only limit myself to saying that Cuba was not responsible for those mistakes. However, a difficult, complex, and critical situation arose as a consequence of an enormous military escalation by South Africa, which intervened because of an offensive the Angolan forces were carrying out in a faraway region of southeastern Angola against the forces that are fighting the government of Angola, against the UNITA forces.

Powerful Angolan forces had gathered there, in an area that is far from the edge of the strategic line that our troops were defending. And the South Africans intervened because of this Angolan military operation, not far from the northeastern border of Namibia. They intervened with their tanks, infantry, planes, and Namibian mercenary forces, and they created a difficult situation. They dealt military blows to the Angolans, who were left without food, fuel, or ammunition south of the Longa River.

That was when the Angolan retreat began. The same thing had already happened once before, in 1985, when the South Africans openly intervened. But in 1985 they repelled the Angolan offensive, on Angolan territory. Keep in mind that all this is in Angolan territory, and the South African military operations were carried out in Angolan territory.

But this time they pursued the Angolan forces and besieged them at Cuito Cuanavale. There were thousands and thousands of men from Angola's best units and they were in danger of being wiped out. That would have been disastrous for Angola; it would have meant the possibility of destroying the independence of Angola and its revolution.

The Angolans requested our help, and our help was essential—essential!—for either the help was given or the efforts made throughout the years were lost. But moreover, help was essential not only to collaborate with Angola to get out of a difficult situation, but also for the security of our own troops. We drew the conclusion that if South Africa were allowed to carry out that operation, to wipe out the Angolan troops, the situation could become dangerous for our own troops as well. Therefore, without hesitation, the leadership of the party decided to help the Angolans resolve that situation.

But it was impossible to do so without reinforcements. The troops that had been in Angola for years were not enough to guard a long strategic line and also resolve the situation that had been created in Cuito Cuanavale. That's why we had to reinforce the troops. But this kind of operation cannot be done only partially. How many troops had to be sent to Angola? All that we needed to resolve the situation. They could not be small groups of reinforcements but all the reinforcements necessary.

For years the South African enemy had been superior in men and had a favorable relationship of forces. The relationship of forces had to be changed, and once again our people had to carry out a feat, and they did so. I said our people, for our people are really the heart and soul of our Revolutionary Armed Forces. [*Applause*]

It was really impressive to see how our soldiers, the reserves, the units responded. It was truly impressive—despite the fact that we've been fulfilling this mission for years. An action of this kind does not depend on techniques, on money, on resources, or anything else; it depends on the human factor. And the human factor was decisive.

You have just seen a documentary that explains a lot about it, that's why I don't have to say too much. Of course, we followed certain principles: it was necessary to choose the field of action, not to act where it was most favorable for the enemy, but where it was most favorable for our forces.

The South Africans had chosen Cuito Cuanavale as the field of action, a faraway place, where logistics becomes extremely difficult. They had chosen that field; we had to draw up another strategy. We had to accept the challenge of Cuito to keep them there, to stop them. We had to get into Cuito to support the Angolan forces and, at their side, wage the historic battle of Cuito Cuanavale, where the enemy was stopped, where it really smashed up against the Angolan-Cuban resistance. I believe that it was truly a historic battle of great importance. Some day it will be put down in writing and much more will be said about it.

But the essence of the Cuban-Angolan strategy was the advance in the western region of the southern front. In this way the Cuban and Angolan forces advanced more than 250 kilometers toward the border with Namibia without stopping, creating a new situation.

Everything that was done in Cuito Cuanavale, as well as in the western part of the southern front, could never have been achieved on a solid basis without the reinforcements sent from Cuba. They were essential. A powerful force was created. Therefore the relationship of forces changed in southern Angola, it changed in our favor. [*Applause*]

I must say that in Cuito Cuanavale as well as in the western part of the southern front, the Angolan soldiers—who are so accustomed to our company, so closely bound to us—maintained an exemplary conduct, a heroic conduct, an extraordinary conduct. [*Applause*] The military situation changed completely.

On advancing more than 200 kilometers, our armored units, which were strongly supported by antiaircraft weapons, were getting far from our air bases. We had to build an air base as fast as we could, and I can tell you with satisfaction that if there was ever a place where a greater effort was made than the one we have seen here in our country during the last few days, it was there in Cahama. In a matter of weeks, our troops and construction workers built an airstrip 3,500 meters long, and since one was not enough, in a matter of weeks a second one was built, [*Applause*] with concrete and all—the parts had to be made of concrete—apart from those made with asphalt; with all the shelters for the planes and all the necessary installations for the base.

Yesterday, the southern front military command sent us a telegram saying that in tribute to July 26, the second airstrip had been finished. [*Applause*] So they achieved not only a military feat, but also a construction feat. Our powerful forces, reinforced with antiaircraft weapons, with air support, began taking all the necessary fortification measures against any type of surprise, against any enemy attack by air or land. Thus the Cuban-Angolan troops advanced until they were near the Namibian border. There the really experienced, powerful units have been concentrated, with a tremendously high morale.

But our objective was not to achieve a humiliating and destructive military victory over our enemy. If we had to wage the battle, then we had to be ready to do so with all the conditions for success and for victory, which are the conditions that were created there. But we were not seeking military glory, or military victory; we were seeking a political, just solution to the conflict. That was the main objective, and that's why the possibilities of negotiation were not discarded. The alternatives for a negotiated political solution were not discarded and we worked seriously and responsibly to take advantage of the slightest possibility of a solution of that kind.

We had to act calmly and serenely, for whenever such powerful forces meet, the leaders and those responsible have to be more serene than ever. They must act cold-bloodedly. That's why we also worked in the diplomatic field. Achieving the objective with no bloody battles was already an extraordinary success. To do so from so far away and with a minimum of casualties was a real feat politically and militarily. The precision and efficiency with which our troops advanced on the southern front was really impressive, as was the way they thwarted the enemy's action in Cuito Cuanavale. It was necessary to run risks, and we did, but we are really on the threshold of a political solution. We have come a long way.

The people have been quite well informed concerning the military situation through the documentary and through what has been published on the agreements in New York. The bases for a political solution already exist and progress is being made. Therefore there is a real possibility of finding a just, dignified, and honorable solution for all those concerned that includes the security of Angola and the independence of Namibia. [*Applause*] On the basis of this overall solution, Cuba and Angola will be ready to—and in fact, if the agreement is fulfilled, if the agreement is achieved, if the agreement is signed, in common agreement, Cuba and Angola will proceed to gradually and totally withdraw the contingent of Cuban internationalist forces from Angola. [*Applause*]

The withdrawal cannot be abrupt. There is a minimum of time that is necessary for the Angolans to take over the areas, the installations, the positions we defend. But based on the principles and the points included in the agreement, our military presence will no longer be needed in Angola.

We are working seriously and we will strictly abide by whatever is agreed to. The fulfillment of this historic and honorable mission as a test of firmness and tenacity will soon have lasted thirteen years.

It was possible not only because of the merits of our party, but mainly because of the merits of our people. Such loyalty, such willpower is possible only when one can rely on a people like ours. So when the time comes when our mission is considered complete, we will gladly welcome our troops back; we will gladly welcome those who built our fortifications and military bases; we will gladly welcome our brave army when it returns to our homeland; we will gladly welcome the tens upon tens upon tens of thousands of men who will then take part in this other colossal battle, the battle to develop our country, the battle to strengthen our revolution. [*Applause*]

Perhaps the most outstanding thing about all these years is that they were difficult years, years when very big efforts proved necessary to strengthen the country's defense, when it became necessary to conceive and organize a strategy calling for the war of the entire people. Perhaps no one ever thought that a country directly threatened by imperialism like Cuba would remain loyal to the fulfillment of those international obligations. Perhaps no one ever thought that a country as threatened as Cuba would be able to ship out the combat gear it shipped to Angola, because that's where many of our antiaircraft weapons, our most modern antiaircraft weapons are.

Now, why were we able to do so? Why were we able to ship out tens of thousands of fighters, hundreds of tanks, guns, and so forth? Why? Because we had the people with us, because our conception of the war of the entire people makes us very strong, because the defense of the country is in the hands of the entire people! And only a people with that spirit, with such a conception could be able to accomplish the feat of remaining faithful to those commitments and shipping out the reinforcements sent over without fear or hesitation. Because had imperialism wanted opportunistically to take advantage of that situation to attack our country, it would have clashed with our people here and would have experienced—we're certain of it—another Girón [Bay of Pigs], two Giróns, three Giróns, 100 Giróns.[9] [*Applause*]

This is what I can tell you.

Our duty, from this podium, on this thirty-fifth anniversary, is not to fan animosity or passion, to be careful rather than boastful, to refrain from using triumphant language. We are confident we're headed along the right road to peace, yet we'll remain alert, we'll remain strong, and we'll go on strengthening ourselves right up to the minute the negotiated peace agreement is signed. Then we'll be able to say that the problem has truly been solved. [*Applause*]

To the people of Santiago de Cuba I ask that they carry on, that they go on working as they've done so far. Awaiting them are the thirtieth anniversary of the triumph of the revolution and the fourth party congress. Let the city of Santiago de Cuba be worthy of creating the atmosphere, the spirit, the optimism, and the zeal that ought to permeate the Fourth Congress, where a full account can be rendered of the rectification effort we're now carrying out and the advances we have set our sights on and the accomplishments we're making.

I think it will be hard to find a better audience, a better city, a better people, a better spirit to hold a congress to be attended by guests from all the world's revolutionary, Marxist, socialist, progressive, and democratic organizations.

We're already working feverishly on the construction of the auditorium for the congress, we're already working feverishly on the construction of the hotel and many other buildings. That auditorium will be one of the country's finest. That hotel will be for international and domestic tourism, also as one of the country's finest. They won't be the only projects—there are many others, some known and others in the drawing-board stage. I'm certain that there will be some surprises—there will be more things than those mentioned—and that the entire country will make big efforts to cooperate with Santiago de Cuba in making the preparations for that historic event, not only in honor of Santiago but also of Granma Province, which shared with us the battlefield of all that past fighting. It will also be in honor of the remaining eastern provinces, which formerly were one single province; it will be in honor of the entire country.

It was not by chance, compañeras and compañeros of Santiago de Cuba, that the eastern provinces were chosen to stage the start of the last war of liberation of our nation. It was in the eastern provinces that the first war of independence began; it was in the eastern provinces that the insurmountable deed of heroism, the Baraguá Protest, took place. It was in the eastern provinces that the second war of independence began, the so-called Little War. It was in the eastern provinces that the third war of independence began.[10] It was in the eastern provinces that José Martí shed his blood. It was in the eastern provinces where throughout history our people waged countless struggles. It was in the eastern provinces where the nation's last war of liberation started on July 26, 1953. It was in the eastern provinces where the November 30 uprising, the *Granma* landing, the Sierra Maestra epic and the Second Front of Oriente took place. It was from the eastern provinces that the glorious columns led by Camilo Cienfuegos and Che Guevara started out toward central and western Cuba.[11] [*Applause*]

Concerning the nation's preparedness for defense and the fulfillment of internationalist missions, it makes us proud to think that this new generation of easterners now has more than 6,000 residents of Santiago de Cuba—6,000 sons and daughters of this province—fulfilling internationalist missions at this time, plus 24,000 sons and daughters of the other eastern provinces, fulfilling internationalist missions, most of them on Angola's southern front. [*Applause*] Such are the fruits of the Moncada attack, such are the marvelous young people in the new generation who are now re-enacting and rebuilding the Moncada garrison, the November 30 uprising, the *Granma* expedition, the fighting in the Sierra Maestra January 1, October 10, and February 24;[12] the ones at the forefront, at the vanguard. And we all hope that in honor of Cuba, in honor of our people, they will go on being at the vanguard of our struggles for freedom, our struggles for justice, our struggles for socialism!

Patria o muerte! [Homeland or death]

Venceremos! [We will win]

[*Ovation*]

NOTES

1. The normal Cuban workweek is Monday through Friday plus every other Saturday. Cubans have an annual one-month vacation.

2. Cuban dictator Gerardo Machado, who was overthrown by a popular upsurge in 1933.

3. On March 10, 1952, Fulgencio Batista staged a coup d'état against the Cuban government then in power, suspended all constitutional guarantees, and established a military dictatorship.

4. José Martí, Cuban national hero, organized the Cuban Revolutionary Party and launched the 1895 war of independence against Spain. He was killed in battle the same year.

5. The term *mambí* refers to Cuban fighters in the independence wars against Spain.

6. People's Power is the Cuban system of representative assemblies on the municipal, provincial, and national levels. At the municipal level, delegates are chosen in popular elections that must have at least two candidates nominated by community meetings.

7. In 1981, Cuba was hit by an epidemic of dengue fever. Tens of thousands came down with the illness, with over 150 deaths, mostly of children. Cuba's immediate and massive response, however, was able to rapidly bring the epidemic under control and save countless lives.

8. Esteban Lazo Hernández is the first secretary of the Communist Party of Cuba in Santiago de Cuba Province and a member of the party's Political Bureau.

9. In April 1961, 1,500 Cuban-born mercenaries organized by the U.S. government invaded Cuba at the Bay of Pigs. After seventy-two hours, the last invaders surrendered at Playa Girón (Girón Beach), which is the name Cubans use for the entire battle.

10. Cuba's three independence wars against Spain were the Ten Years War of 1868–78 (followed by Cuban Gen. Antonio Maceo's celebrated "Baraguá Protest" against the peace treaty ending that war), the "Little War" of 1879, and the conflict of 1895–98 that ended in Spain's defeat.

11. November 30, 1956, was the date of an uprising in Santiago de Cuba timed to coincide with the arrival of the *Granma*. The Second Front of Oriente was a guerrilla column formed in 1958 under the command of Raúl Castro, operating in the mountains to the north of Santiago de Cuba. In mid-1958, Camilo Cienfuegos and Ernesto Che Guevara, both central commanders of the Rebel Army, led guerrilla columns westward from the Sierra Maestra mountains in eastern Cuba to the central part of the island, a move that was decisive to the revolution's victory.

12. On January 1, 1959, Batista fled Cuba, marking the triumph of the revolution; October 10, 1868, was the date of the beginning of Cuba's first war of independence; February 24, 1895, marked the beginning of the final independence war against Spain.

CUBA'S SOCIALIST REVOLUTION

Women in Cuba: The Making of a Revolution Within the Revolution
VILMA ESPÍN
ASELA DE LOS SANTOS
YOLANDA FERRER

The integration of women in the ranks and leadership of the Cuban Revolution was intertwined with the proletarian course led by Fidel Castro from the start. This is the story of that revolution and how it transformed the women and men who made it. $17. Also in Spanish, Farsi, Greek.

Cuba and the Coming American Revolution
JACK BARNES

This is a book about the example set by the Cuban people that socialist revolution is not only necessary—it can be made. A book about the struggles of workers and other exploited producers in the imperialist heartland, and the youth attracted to them. About the class struggle in the US, where the revolutionary capacities of working people are as utterly discounted by the ruling powers as were those of the Cuban toilers. And just as wrongly. $10. Also in Spanish, French, Farsi.

How Far We Slaves Have Come!
South Africa and Cuba in Today's World
NELSON MANDELA, FIDEL CASTRO

Speaking together in Cuba in 1991, Mandela and Castro discuss the role of Cuba in the history of Africa and Angola's victory over the invading US-backed South African army. That victory accelerated the fight to bring down the racist apartheid system. $7. Also in Spanish and Farsi.

PATHFINDERPRESS.COM

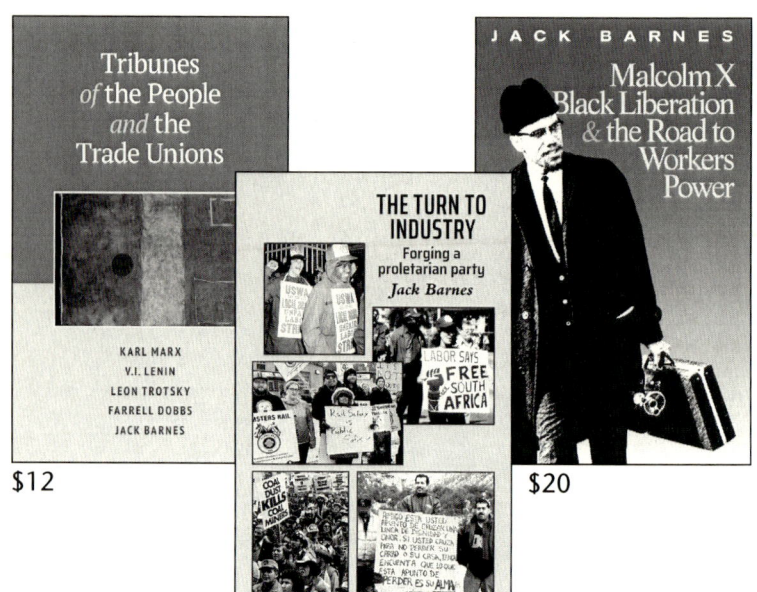

$12 $20

$15

Three books to be read as one …

about building a party that's working class in program, composition, and action. One that recognizes, in word and deed, the most revolutionary fact of our time …

… that working people have the power to create a different world as we act together to defend our own class interests—not those of the privileged classes who exploit our labor, not of those who fear us as "deplorables," or just plain "trash."

As we advance along a revolutionary course toward workers power, we will transform ourselves and awaken to our own worth. Also in Spanish, French, Farsi, Greek.

Special Offer!
All three $30

The Turn to Industry and *Tribunes of the People and the Trade Unions* $20

Either book plus *Malcolm X, Black Liberation, and the Road to Workers Power* $25

CAPITALIST CRISIS AND THE FIGHT FOR WORKERS POWER

Are They Rich Because They're Smart?
Class, Privilege, and Learning Under Capitalism

JACK BARNES

Exposes growing class inequalities in the US and the self-serving rationalizations of well-paid professionals who think their "brilliance" equips them to "regulate" working people, who don't know what's in our own best interest. $10. Also in Spanish, French, Farsi, Arabic, Greek.

The Clintons' Anti-Working-Class Record
Why Washington Fears Working People

JACK BARNES

What working people need to know about the profit-driven course of Democrats and Republicans alike over the last three decades. And the political awakening of workers seeking to understand and resist the capitalist rulers' assaults. $10. Also in Spanish, French, Farsi, Greek.

Is Socialist Revolution in the US Possible?
A Necessary Debate Among Working People

MARY-ALICE WATERS

An unhesitating "Yes"—that's the answer given here. Possible—but not inevitable. That depends on what working people *do*. $7. Also in Spanish, French, Farsi.

PATHFINDERPRESS.COM

THE WORKING CLASS AND THE FIGHT AGAINST JEW-HATRED

New!
The Fight Against Jew-Hatred and Pogroms in the Imperialist Epoch
Stakes for the International Working Class
V.I. LENIN, LEON TROTSKY
FARRELL DOBBS, JAMES P. CANNON
JACK BARNES, DAVE PRINCE

Jew-hatred and pogroms—such as Hamas carried out on October 7, 2023—are now part of the permanent social convulsions and wars of the imperialist epoch. The authors explain why fighting Jew-hatred is of decisive importance to the working class and oppressed nations of the world. They answer the question: *What is to be done to end it*—for all time. $10. Also in Spanish, French, Greek.

Imperialism's March Toward Fascism and War
JACK BARNES

"There will be new Hitlers, new Mussolinis. That is inevitable. What is not inevitable is that they will triumph. The working-class vanguard will organize our class to fight back against the devastating toll we are made to pay for the capitalist crisis. The future of humanity will be decided in the contest between these contending class forces." In *New International* no. 10. $14. Also in Spanish, French, Farsi, Greek.

The Jewish Question
A Marxist Interpretation
ABRAM LEON

The battle against reactionary forces aiming to exterminate the Jews remains central to world politics, as shown by the genocidal October 2023 pogrom in Israel. Why is Jew-hatred still raising its ugly head? What are its class roots? Why, as Abram Leon explains, is there no solution "independent of the world proletarian revolution"? Revised translation, new introduction, 40 pages of illustrations and maps. $17. Also in Spanish, French, Greek.

WOMEN'S EMANCIPATION AND THE WORKING CLASS

New Expanded Edition!
Cosmetics, Fashion, and the Exploitation of Women
MARY-ALICE WATERS
JOSEPH HANSEN, EVELYN REED

"Norms of beauty and fashion are inseparable from the class struggle" is the new opening chapter of this timely expanded edition of a lively 1950s debate in the *Militant*, a socialist newsweekly. How cosmetics and fashion monopolies rake in profits from social insecurities of women and adolescents. Why women's integration in the workforce and unions marks a major advance in the fight for their emancipation. A Marxist classic on the origins of women's oppression and the working-class road forward. $15. Also in Spanish, French, Farsi, Greek.

The Origin of the Family, Private Property, and the State
FREDERICK ENGELS

The emergence of class-divided society gave rise to repressive state bodies and the oppression of women to enable the ruling classes to pass along wealth and privilege. Engels discusses the consequences for working people of these class institutions—from their ancient forms to their modern versions. $15. Also in Spanish and Farsi.

Women's Liberation and the African Freedom Struggle
THOMAS SANKARA

"There is no true social revolution without the liberation of women," explains the leader of the 1983–87 revolution in the West African country of Burkina Faso. $5. Also in Spanish, French, Farsi.

PATHFINDERPRESS.COM

ALSO FROM PATHFINDER

The Low Point of Labor Resistance Is Behind Us
The Socialist Workers Party Looks Forward

JACK BARNES
MARY-ALICE WATERS
STEVE CLARK

The global order imposed by Washington after its victory in World War II is shattering. A long retreat by the working class and unions has come to an end. The bosses and their government are stepping up attacks on our wages, conditions, and constitutional rights. This book highlights opportunities for building a mass proletarian party able to lead the struggle to end capitalist rule, opening a socialist future for humanity. $10. Also in Spanish, French, Greek.

Thomas Sankara Speaks
The Burkina Faso Revolution, 1983–87

Under Sankara's guidance, Burkina Faso's revolutionary government led peasants, workers, women, and youth to expand literacy; to sink wells, plant trees, erect housing; to combat women's oppression; to carry out land reform; to join others worldwide to free themselves from the imperialist yoke. $20. Also in French.

Teamster Rebellion
FARRELL DOBBS

The 1934 strikes that won union recognition for truckers and warehouse workers in Minneapolis and helped pave the way for the working-class social movement that built the industrial unions. The first of four volumes by a central leader of these battles. $16. Also in Spanish, French, Farsi, Greek.